John Wayne

LESSONS FOR MY CHILDREN

John Wayne with his youngest son Ethan on the set of *The Sons of Katie Elder* (1965).

FOREWORD
By Ethan Wayne

When I think of my father, something that stands out very clearly is his belief that if you're going to take the time and energy to do something, you should do it right. I remember having to sweep our yard when I was probably 7 years old—the yard was huge and there were all these seeds that fell out of the rubber trees everywhere. One day I was sweeping kind of lazily, and my father came out and took the broom from me and said, "This is how you sweep properly." It wasn't so much about him teaching me his specific sweeping technique though, it was more him saying in a general sense, "If you're going to do it, do it."

That notion bled into all aspects of his life, and it ended up coming into ours because we lived with him.

Even when we spent our free time on the *Wild Goose*, it was kind of like a project. We'd go swimming, hiking, exploring, fishing, diving for abalone—morning to night, there was activity. He was always somewhere and always doing something. He might be filming in Durango, Mexico, then have to come back to Los Angeles to receive the Academy Award, then go back to Durango, Mexico, to finish the film. Then he might get on his boat in Acapulco and sail south along the mainland, then get on someone's plane to go to Monterey for something there. My father had a lot going on, he had a lot of ground to cover, but he was always doing everything to the fullest extent— and instilled an appreciation for that approach to life in all of his children.

I think about these little memories of my dad often. And though they weren't necessarily presented as such at the time, they have grown into important life lessons for me over the years. Maybe that's because I lost my father at such a young age, or maybe that's the way he planned it. Now, as you read these memories my siblings and I have of our father as well as anecdotes and quotes from his film career and personal life, my hope is his example will inspire you and those you hold dear. Whether you choose to apply them to your own life as a parent or pass them down to your children and grandchildren, you'll be carrying on Duke's legacy. And for that, my family and I thank you.

—ETHAN WAYNE

John Wayne with
his son Michael and
daughter Toni.

TABLE OF
CONTENTS

WORK

Duke knew if you were going to do a job, you had to do it right.

A tailor mends John Wayne's shirt on the set of *Red River* (1948).

"He was driven from the day he was born to succeed. He wanted to attend the U.S. Naval Academy, but he wasn't accepted because his family didn't have the connections. But his football abilities earned him a scholarship at USC, until he broke his shoulder surfing and was unable to play football. He lost his scholarship and couldn't afford school, so he went to work. If he had gone to the Naval Academy, he would have been the head of the Joint Chiefs of Staff. If he had graduated from college, he would've been president of the United States. But as it happened, he gravitated toward the film business and became a huge star. He was going to succeed no matter where he landed, and he used that drive to motivate his work ethic."

—Patrick Wayne

John Wayne and his son Patrick on the set of *Rio Bravo* (1959).

John Wayne
and Marguerite
Churchill in *The
Big Trail* (1930).

ACT
NATURALLY

Duke's inexperience on the screen
worked in his favor for *The Big Trail*,
as director Raoul Walsh told the
studio, "I don't want an actor."

"No great trail was ever built without hardship."

—Breck Coleman,
The Big Trail (1930)

SUCCEED OUTSIDE OF YOUR COMFORT ZONE

Before he was a Western icon, John Wayne was finding his way in Hollywood by taking any role he could. As a result, the young actor found himself playing unconventional roles and performing tasks for which he wasn't naturally suited. Whether it was learning to skate to play a hockey star in *Idol of the Crowds* or having to lip-sync to pass as a singing cowboy in *Riders of Destiny*, Duke not only did what he had to do to get by, he did it to the best of his ability. And Hollywood took notice. His relentless desire to do whatever was asked of him led directly to his breakout in *Stagecoach*. Had he not honed his skills making a decade's worth of B movies, he may have never gotten there.

John Wayne shakes hands with Hal Neiman in *Idol of the Crowds* (1937).

GET IT DONE

Not only did Duke have to learn to skate for *Idol of the Crowds*, he had to do so in one day's time as the ice rink was only rented for 24 hours.

John Wayne as
Ethan Edwards in
The Searchers (1956).

"Well, you like each picture for a different reason. But I think my favorite will always be the next one."

—John Wayne

"He didn't have access to acting schools, but he worked in so many films that it was like going to acting school. He would work and then he would look at the film and decide if what he was trying to do was coming across on the screen. If it wasn't, he would think of what he could do to change that. He worked his trade, and he worked it well."

—Patrick Wayne

Duke and Patrick Wayne on the set of *The Green Berets* (1968).

Toni, Patrick, Duke, Melinda and Michael on the set of *The Quiet Man* (1952).

A FAMILY BUSINESS

Duke's children Toni, Patrick, Melinda and Michael all appeared as extras in their father's classic film *The Quiet Man* (1952).

RESPONSIBILITY BEFORE REWARD

"When he filmed *The Quiet Man* in Ireland in 1951, he had a big house there, so we kids would come stay with him. As we got off the plane in Shannon, he said, 'I know you're going to want to buy gifts and take stuff home, but you've got to earn the money.' So at 10 years old, I was thinking, 'Oh my God, I've got to get a job!' The next morning, at 6 a.m., I walked a mile or so to the town and got a man to hire me to sweep. When I got back to the house, everyone was in a panic. They said, 'We thought you were kidnapped!' My dad was sitting at the dining room table, very calm, and he said: 'Nice of you to show up for breakfast. Where have you been?' Well, now I was crying. 'I went and got a job, like you said.' He said: 'You what? I meant here! On the set! To be in the crowd scenes!'"

—Melinda Wayne

LOOK OUT FOR
THE LITTLE GUY

Even before he was a huge star, John
Wayne was using his burgeoning status
to lift up those he worked with. Actress
Lorna Gray, Duke's costar in 1938's *Red
River Range*, recalled the star being
"terribly, terribly nice," as he patiently
helped her learn to handle her horse.
During the same production, Duke also
intentionally tripped numerous times
while shooting a scene, forcing a series
of reshoots and helping the crew on the
set earn overtime pay. No matter your
role in any workplace, you'll find it's
more enjoyable and more productive
when everyone around you is given the
chance to thrive.

HELP WHERE YOU CAN

In a biography, Lorna Gray attributed her eventual success to the patience and help she received from Duke on *Red River Range*.

John Wayne and
Patrick Wayne in
the 1956 classic
The Searchers.

"He was a professional to a fault—he was on time, he knew his lines and he was prepared for anything he needed to do. If there was some physical activity that was required of him, he was prepared. If he was supposed to be a skilled blacksmith in the film, he knew how to look like he knew what he was doing in the scene. He was ready to work from the first moment of the day until the last moment of the wrap."

—Patrick Wayne

DO IT YOURSELF

While filming *Angel and the Badman* in 1946, John Wayne dove deep into the history and lore of Texas and became particularly inspired by the story of the Alamo. Davy Crockett's incredible heroism immediately struck the actor as the type of story that belonged on the big screen, and he was determined to make it happen. When studio execs refused to budge over budgets and creative control, the legend remained undeterred. He put his own production company behind the project, betting on the project with his own money and working tirelessly to bring the ambitious film to life. Finally in 1960, Duke saw his dream come true when *The Alamo* premiered in San Antonio, Texas. Had he relied on others to get it done, it might have never seen the light of day.

John Wayne and his daughter Aissa on the set of *The Alamo*, c. 1959.

Duke and Ethan on the set of John Wayne's 1968 film *Hellfighters*.

"I spent a lot of time with my father on location when I was a young boy—and at least while I was around, he seemed the most happy when he was focused on a project. We'd get to the set and he'd be one of the first people, if not the first person, there. And after a full day of work we'd go back to the hotel room and I just remember that script was always in his hand. He'd get in bed and the last hour of his day was spent looking at that script and making notes. When I was a kid, it was just like 'Dad reading his thing before bed,' but as an adult I realize how focused he was on it. The way he lived his life was exactly the work ethic you'd imagine for John Wayne. Sure he had a good time, but when he was working, he was very focused. All the stuff he would do when he wasn't on a job, all those distractions were gone, and it was pretty much that story from when he woke up until he went to sleep."

—Ethan Wayne

WORK WON'T WAIT FOR YOU

John Wayne's lung cancer diagnosis in 1964 could have easily spelled the end of his career. The star had to undergo major surgery to remove one of his lungs and a few ribs, which jeopardized his role in *The Sons of Katie Elder.* Rather than allow another actor to replace him in the role, John Wayne returned to work the moment his body allowed it. From there, he went on to turn in several more classic performances well into the next decade, proving not even "the Big C" could slow him down. Duke knew better than anyone that the things we work so hard to build can easily slip away if our grip ever gets too loose.

Earl Holliman, John Wayne, Michael Anderson Jr., director Henry Hathaway and Dean Martin on the set of *The Sons of Katie Elder* (1965).

SET THE RECORD STRAIGHT

Before returning to work, Duke held a press conference regarding his cancer recovery in an effort to be transparent with the public.

Duke and Patrick on the set of *The Comancheros* (1961).

LEARN RIGHT
AND LEARN FAST

"On *The Comancheros* with my dad, I had to do a horseback riding scene, and when the dailies came back they looked awful. I didn't look good on the horse, though I knew how to ride. My dad came back and said, 'You're going to ride a horse and look good doing it if you're going to be in this business.' Now, I'd grown up riding horses [in] films, but there's a difference between knowing how to ride a horse and looking good doing it, and I was supposed to be a Texas ranger. Riding a horse [properly] means spending a lot of time—it's a combination of weight and balance and you have to kind of roll. We shot the sequence again and everything was fine. It was a conscious effort to make it look natural—and it doesn't happen in an instant."

—Patrick Wayne

"If I depended on the critics' judgment and recognition, I'd never have gone into the motion-picture business."

—John Wayne

John Wayne and
Marguerite Churchill in
The Big Trail (1930)

KEEP ON
KEEPIN' ON

Even though the first film he
starred in was a financial failure,
John Wayne stuck with the acting
business until he found success.

John Wayne
has a laugh during
the filming of *The
Undefeated* (1969).

ADAPT AS NECESSARY

After an injury restricted use of his
arm on the set of *The Undefeated*,
Duke kept shooting and was filmed
at strategic angles as a workaround.

KNOW WHEN TO SAY NO

While he wasn't afforded such a luxury in the early years of his career, John Wayne was able to maintain his status in Hollywood by turning down roles that weren't right for him. When legendary director Mel Brooks approached the Western icon about playing the part of the Waco Kid in the cowboy comedy *Blazing Saddles*, Duke knew he had to turn the offer down. According to Brooks, the star said the role was too raunchy for him to take, though he would be first in line to see it at the theater. As John Wayne proved, knowing exactly who you are and what you stand for is one of the secrets to success.

GIVE YOUR ALL, ALWAYS

For as long as John Wayne lived, the movie-going public's demand for his films never ceased. And fortunately for his fans, Duke had no interest in retirement. "As long as people want to pay money to see me act, I'll keep on making Westerns until the day I die," the icon once said. Even as age and health complications began to catch up to him, John Wayne kept this promise to the people who made his life and career possible. Work will inevitably consume much of your time and energy, but there's always value to be found in a job well done—especially when you know your efforts are impacting others.

John Wayne
as J.B. Books in
The Shootist (1976).

FAMILY

Duke's number one priority was being the kind of father his children could always look up to.

John Wayne reads a *Prince Valiant* comic with his children Patrick, Melinda, Toni and Michael.

John Wayne
embraces his
daughter Marisa.

"We had a rule in the house: I was not allowed to walk by him without giving him a hug. I would play a game like I was trying to sneak by him and he would say, 'I see you, get over here!' He was a very affectionate, kind, funny father."

—Marisa Wayne

"I've always followed my father's advice: He told me, first, to always keep my word and, second, to never insult anybody unintentionally. And, third, he told me not to go around looking for trouble."

—John Wayne

Duke, his younger brother Robert and their father Clyde Morrison.

WHATEVER IT TAKES

To promote *The Sons of Katie Elder*, Duke stepped out of his comfort zone to sing a song on Dean Martin's variety series.

John Wayne, Dean Martin, Earl Holliman and Michael Anderson Jr. in *The Sons of Katie Elder* (1965).

IN TOUGH TIMES, TURN TO FAMILY

The Sons of Katie Elder (1965) stars John Wayne as John Elder, a rugged gunslinger who reunites with his mostly disparate brothers ahead of their mother's funeral. Though the brothers bicker, their familial bond quickly overrides their differences as they unite to honor their mother's memory and avenge their father's murder. The film is a stirring reminder of the importance of family and how hardship, heartache and grief can be conquered so long as we aren't afraid to lean on the people we care about.

"With his kids, he lived his life by example. It was kind of like: 'Choose whatever you want to choose. This is how I live my life, and if it works for you, fine.' The things that were important to him were the core values of trustworthiness, reliability, friendship, accountability and responsibility. He would talk about these things peripherally, giving us parameters for behavior that always included holding yourself accountable and responsible."

—Patrick Wayne

John Wayne and Patrick on the set of *Rio Grande* (1950).

John Wayne poses with four generations of his family for a photo. His mother, Mary "Molly" Brown, is in the center.

ALWAYS MAKE TIME FOR MOM

Even well after his career took off, John Wayne remained very close to his mother and often invited her to join him on the sets of his films.

"I have tried to live my life so that my family would love me and my friends respect me. The others can do whatever the hell they please."

—John Wayne

RESPECT YOUR ELDERS

"I had clothes all over the floor [of my room on the *Wild Goose*]. And after asking me about five times, I woke up to him throwing everything overboard. It all came down to disrespect, and in his mind it was disrespectful that I wasn't picking up after myself. And as a parent now, I have a real hard time when one of my kids rolls his or her eyes at me."

—Marisa Wayne

John Wayne
and Marisa
Wayne aboard
the *Wild Goose.*

TAKE A CHANCE
NOW AND THEN

In *The Cowboys* (1972), rancher
Wil Andersen hires a group of
schoolboys who, despite their age,
become capable ranch hands.

"Every man wants his children to be better than he was."

—Wil Andersen,
The Cowboys (1972)

"I am a demonstrative man, a baby picker-upper, a hugger and a kisser—that's my nature."

—John Wayne

John Wayne with his youngest son Ethan in Hawaii.

Duke and his youngest daughter, Marisa, who still looks up to her dad.

"When it came to teaching a lesson, the punishment was quick and then it was immediately: 'Come over here and give me a hug. Now we're going to move forward.' He didn't hold a grudge, he didn't make you feel bad for days. Now I have two kids, and it's really hard because you don't want to discipline them but you also want to leave an impression. And then you need to let it go."

—Marisa Wayne

FUN

Since his spare time was so sparse, John Wayne knew the importance of having a good time.

Duke plays with his dogs at his home in San Fernando Valley, California, c. 1952

"Most of his free time was spent bird hunting, fishing or just exploring. He liked mining; some of his buddies were into that. It wasn't like when he wasn't working he was home doing nothing. He was usually active somewhere, usually outdoors doing something at least a little adventurous, and it was always with good friends."

—Ethan Wayne

Duke and Ethan Wayne spend time together on the *Wild Goose*.

Patrick and John Wayne on the set of the 1955 film *The Sea Chase*.

BROADEN YOUR HORIZONS

John Wayne's home library featured everything from poetry books about the American West to historical fiction by Sir Arthur Conan Doyle.

"Sometimes you'd be the object of a joke, but it was always an expression of affection. Once when my youngest sister was on the *Wild Goose*, she had these decals, and my dad took one of them and stuck it on the side of the ship. He called her over and said, 'Aissa, what is the meaning of this?' pointing to the decal. She was totally innocent saying, 'I have no idea!' He played this out for a while but then we all had a big laugh about it."

—Patrick Wayne

FUN IS WHAT YOU MAKE IT

Few Hollywood friendships in history can rival that of John Wayne and Ward Bond. Not only did the duo go back as far as their time on the gridiron at USC, they also had very unique ways of having a good time together. The two became known for their behind-the-scenes antics, which often involved sharing drinks and jokes. On some occasions, Duke and Bond would even get into knock-down, drag-out fistfights just for the fun of it. It may not have been everyone's idea of a good time, but their incredible closeness proved it was the type of fun best suited for their friendship.

Ward Bond and John Wayne on the set of *The Big Trail* (1930). The film was the pair's sixth together.

John and Marisa Wayne spend time together on the *Wild Goose*.

ALLOW LEGACIES TO LIVE ON

Thanks to Hornblower Cruises, fans of John Wayne can tour the *Wild Goose* and see the bulkheads that were home to so many good times.

"We spent our weekends, school vacations and summers on the *Wild Goose*. That's where he could really unwind and be himself with family and friends. Obviously, it was before Facebook and satellite TV, so we got to do things and really be together, like just sitting down to enjoy a meal. He loved being with his close friends and his kids."

—Marisa Wayne

LEARN TO LAUGH AT YOURSELF

For as serious as he was on the big screen, John Wayne never fancied himself too big of a star to be the butt of a joke. When the satirical *Harvard Lampoon* invited him to attend a ceremony honoring him as its "Man of the Year," Duke took the Ivy Leaguers up on the offer. Not only did he attend the event, John Wayne leaned headlong into his own stereotypes by arriving in an armored tank. Once the festivities began, Duke fully won over the crowd by playing along with jokes about his politics and even his toupee. By being such a good sport, the legend showed us life is simply better when you can laugh at yourself.

John Wayne and Army Reservists of the 178th Infantry Brigade in Harvard Square on January 15, 1974.

187 BDE
D TRP
5 CAV

D 28

JAB WITH A JOKE

When asked if he looked at himself as an "American legend," Duke replied, "Well, not being a Harvard man, I don't look at myself any more than necessary."

HONOR

John Wayne always strived to do the right thing for the right reasons.

John Wayne at home with his awards recognizing decades of inspiring service to the film industry and the people of America.

John Wayne as
J.B. Books in *The
Shootist* (1976).

BE FORTHCOMING

Rather than trying to hide his
illness, Duke openly spoke about his
battle with cancer in various PSAs
and press conferences.

"I won't be wronged, I won't be insulted and I won't be laid a hand on. I don't do these things to other people, and I require the same from them."

—J.B. Books,
The Shootist (1976)

"A man oughta do what he thinks is best."

—Hondo Lane,
Hondo (1953)

John Wayne
and Pal the dog
in *Hondo* (1953).

John Wayne in
costume for
*The Man Who
Shot Liberty
Valance* (1962).

DO GOOD WITHOUT SEEKING GLORY

The thrilling climax of *The Man Who Shot Liberty Valance* (1962) sees Duke's gunslinger Tom Doniphon living up to the film's title by taking out the dastardly Liberty Valance (Lee Marvin). As Ransom Stoddard (James Stewart) finally faces off with the man who has been making his life hell for so long on the darkened main street of town, shots are fired and Valance ends up dead. The bullets that killed the outlaw did not come from Ransom's gun, however, as it was Doniphon who actually fired the fatal shots from the distant shadows. Uninterested in receiving credit for the deed, Doniphon lets Ransom go down in the town's history as "the man who shot Liberty Valance," showing us that sometimes doing the right thing isn't about being rewarded with recognition.

"There's right and there's wrong. You gotta do one or the other."

—Col. Davy Crockett,
The Alamo (1960)

John Wayne as Col. Davy Crockett in *The Alamo* (1960).

John Wayne and Duke the horse in *Ride Him, Cowboy* (1932).

BE KIND TO ALL CREATURES

Duke showed his appreciation for his steeds as chairman for the American Humane Association's "Be Kind to Animals Week" in 1973.

AVOID RASH JUDGMENT

John Wayne's early career film *Ride Him, Cowboy* (1932) sees the soon-to-be superstar as John Drury, seemingly the only man with any sense in town. When a horse named Duke is on trial for murder, Drury tells the townspeople, "Where I come from, we don't shoot horses when they get ornery; we tame 'em." His instincts about Duke's innocence are later proven correct—as it turns out, the horse was framed for murder by an outlaw known as The Hawk (Frank Hagney). Even this early in his career, John Wayne was teaching the importance of justice for all, be it man or beast.

BE UNDERSTANDING OF MISTAKES

"One day when I was about 9, Dad said to me, 'Let's go play some golf.' I figured, well, how hard can it be? So we went out to a driving range, and I'm swinging and swinging and missing the ball. He came around and said, 'Honey, just watch the ball and make contact.' I swung the club and the ball was still there—but I could tell I made contact with something. I turned around and saw my father staggering around. Blood was coming out of the side of his head. And down he went. Whump! A couple of men got an ambulance. When he came to in the hospital, he asked for me. All I could think was, 'I am in so much trouble!' I can still feel it right now, the knot in my stomach. I went in there and all he said was, 'Well, you're the only one who had the nerve to do this to me!' Until that day, he'd always called me Princess. After that, I was Nine Iron, as in, 'Nine Iron, clean up your room!'"

—Marisa Wayne

John Wayne
spends quality
time with his
daughter Marisa.

PATRIOTISM

John Wayne believed the best way to salute your country is to live according to its ideals.

John Wayne sits beside
Old Glory.

Duke and Ethan
on the set of
El Dorado (1967) in
Arizona, c. 1966.

"The world is constantly changing, but I think the character traits he zeroed in on—the things that made the American cowboy iconic— were independence, self-reliance and responsibility. He left us all those messages in his films. He told stories that were uniquely ours. Those are the personality traits of the people who made a difference forging their way out West, regardless of what other people did. The person he was on-screen is somebody we can all look up to."

—Ethan Wayne

"My hope and prayer is that everyone know and love our country for what she really is and what she stands for."

—John Wayne

BE A LOUD AND PROUD PATRIOT

Duke decided to put his love of country on vinyl for all to hear when he recorded the spoken word album *America, Why I Love Her.*

"I don't care whether [my daughter Marisa] ever memorizes the Gettysburg Address or not, but I want her to understand it; and since very few little girls are asked to defend their country, she will probably never have to raise her hand to that oath, but I want her to respect all who do."

—John Wayne, "Why I Am Proud to Be an American" speech, August 1968

STAND UP FOR YOUR BELIEFS

Despite time, circumstances and his own outpost not being on his side, John Wayne's Capt. Kirby York never backs down in 1948's *Fort Apache*. The promotion that should be his instead goes to the younger Lt. Owen Thursday (Henry Fonda), whose approach to dealing with the local Apache tribe is arrogant and wrongheaded. York doesn't allow his status as Thursday's subordinate stop him from letting the lieutenant know how foolish he's being, though, and later opts to take the matter into his own hands.

John Wayne always stood up for his beliefs on and off the big screen, and the self-assured Capt. Kirby York is one of his greatest messengers of that lesson.

John Wayne
and Henry Fonda
in *Fort Apache*
(1948).

John Wayne prepares for battle in *Sands of Iwo Jima* (1949).

YOUR TIME WILL COME

Sands of Iwo Jima earned Duke his first Best Actor Oscar nomination, but it would still be 20 years before the star won the prestigious award.

"**Just give the American people a good cause and there's nothing they can't lick.**"

—John Wayne

"Even when he didn't vote for the president who got elected, he still supported him because that was his president. He always made that clear. With President Carter, he wrote to him and signed a letter, 'From your loyal opposition.' And Carter came to visit him a couple times when he was in the hospital. Even though they had completely different political views, it was a matter of respect."

—Marisa Wayne

John Wayne
and Marisa on
the set of 1968's
Hellfighters.

John Wayne and Mike Henry on the set of *The Green Berets* (1968).

CUT OUT THE MIDDLEMAN

In the 1960s, the Vietnam War was a subject most Hollywood studios were still trying to avoid. John Wayne, however, was eager to tell the stories of the courageous Americans sacrificing everything in the jungles of Southeast Asia, and he planned to do so with a film called *The Green Berets*. Access to military equipment and personnel would be essential to the film's production, so John Wayne opted to go straight to the top with his request. In a personal letter sent directly to President Johnson, Duke outlined his specific needs and his reasoning for making the film. Impressed with his passionate mission, the president and the Pentagon gave the star their full blessing to make *The Green Berets*. Sometimes being direct is the only way to get something done.

SINCERITY

Duke was as honest and straightforward as they come, both on and off the screen.

Duke at the John Wayne Tennis Club in Newport Beach, California, June 8, 1975.

"Words are what men live by...words they say and mean."

—Capt. Jake Cutter,
The Comancheros
(1961)

John Wayne and Ina Balin in *The Comancheros* (1961).

FINISH WHAT YOU STARTED

When director Michael Curtiz had to step away to battle cancer, John Wayne agreed to helm *The Comancheros* to completion.

John Wayne,
in costume for
El Dorado, chats
with Aissa, c. 1966.

KEEPING
'EM CLOSE

Rather than be away from his family
for weeks or months at a time, Duke
often brought his wife and children
with him when filming on location.

THE TRUTH SHALL SET YOU FREE

"I was 5 or 6, playing with a little girl
one day, when I stepped on her head.
On purpose. I was kind of a tomboy, and my dad
liked that. But she went screaming to my dad,
who was inside with some grown-ups.
I followed her in, and my dad, who was
large and loud, demanded, 'Did you step on her
head?' I hesitated, and then he said,
much more quietly: 'Come here.
If you lie to me, you're gonna disappoint me
and you're gonna go to your room
and you're gonna be punished. If you tell the
truth, well, you're still gonna be punished,
but I'm not gonna be disappointed in you.'
I told the truth. And then it was over.
He never rehashed it.
That's the kind of father he was."

—Aissa Wayne

"I've worked in a business where it's almost a requirement to break your word if you want to survive, but whenever I signed a contract for five years or for a certain amount of money, I've always lived up to it."

—John Wayne

John Wayne
has a laugh
while signing
a contract.

John Wayne and
Harry Morgan in
*How the West Was
Won* (1962).

"It doesn't matter what the people think; it's what you think."

—Gen. Sherman,
How the West Was Won (1962)

"I still hear from people of all ages who tell me how much they look up to him, and many of them have a story about how he touched their lives in some way. I've been told, 'My grandmother was down the hall from your father in the hospital and he came down and brought her a cookie.' Every opportunity he had, he made somebody feel special. He really had that personal touch, and it's transcended generations and gone well beyond the movie screen. It wasn't an act—he really was a genuine, great guy."

—Marisa Wayne

Duke and Marisa Wayne share a loving moment.

John Wayne as
Robert Hightower in
3 Godfathers (1948).

"I suppose my best attribute, if you want to call it that, is sincerity. I can sell sincerity because that's the way I am."

—John Wayne

John Wayne as Rooster Cogburn in the 1969 film *True Grit*.

GRIT

Setbacks were mere learning experiences for Duke, who was a true beacon of resiliency.

SETBACKS YIELD NEW OPPORTUNITIES

When Duke entered USC on a
football scholarship, it seemed
his life was all laid out ahead of
him. But as fate would have it, a
bodysurfing injury would leave
the young man sidelined and,
eventually, without a scholarship.
Duke was quick to pull himself up,
though, and soon became a prop
worker for one of Hollywood's most
acclaimed directors, John Ford. The
gig would gradually take him from
propman to extra to leading man to
one of the most iconic stars of all
time—a timeless reminder that even
when you're down, you're never out.

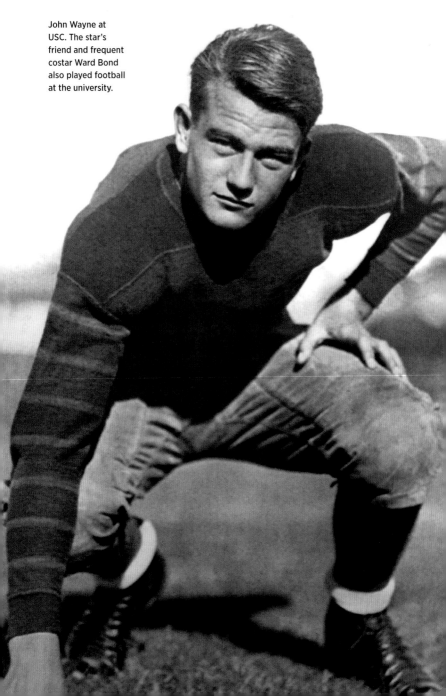

John Wayne at USC. The star's friend and frequent costar Ward Bond also played football at the university.

George Bancroft,
John Wayne and
Louise Platt in
Stagecoach (1939).

PAY YOUR DUES

Prior to landing his big breakout
role in *Stagecoach* (1939),
Duke spent the 1930s honing his
craft in various B Westerns.

"Well, there are some things a man just can't run away from."

—Ringo Kid,
Stagecoach (1939)

"I liked motorcycles. My friend in the neighborhood had a minibike and his dad would take him to races in the desert and I would go with them. One day, I was in a race and I kept hitting this rock that knocked me out of control. When I went to my dad between the two races I said: 'I don't know why I keep hitting this rock. I know it's there, and I'm staring at it, but I hit it every time.' And he said: 'Well, the problem is you're focusing on where you don't wanna go. What you have to do is focus on where you want to go, and you'll go there.' And it worked for me in that race, and it sort of turned into a metaphor for life. It's not about looking where you don't want to go, but looking where you do want to go—in work, relationships, in dealings with yourself."

—Ethan Wayne

John Wayne and
his youngest son
Ethan pose on
three-wheelers.

John Ford and John Wayne on the set of *The Horse Soldiers* (1959). The film is Ford's only feature based on the Civil War.

STAND UP FOR YOURSELF

John Wayne's relationship with his mentor John Ford was not always one of mutual respect and admiration. In his early days working under the director as a propman, Duke was frequently teased by Ford, often in front of other cast and crew members. But one day, when his football past was called into question, the young man seized an opportunity to put a stop to his boss's verbal jabs. Ford challenged Duke to drop to a three-point stance, and then kicked his legs out from under him. Rather than slink away embarrassed, Duke returned to the position and proceeded to tackle the man he would come to know as "Coach." The bold act impressed Ford, and the two became fast friends and even better collaborators from that point on.

THINGS WON'T ALWAYS GO YOUR WAY

"I had just gotten the galleys of *True Grit*. He was in my office, and I was just about to hand him the galleys when the phone rang. It was Henry Hathaway. Before I handed him the phone, I put my hand over the phone and said: 'I'm on this *True Grit* project. Don't commit to it.'

Hathaway started talking to him about *True Grit*—he and Hal Wallis were bidding on it and so forth. When the conversation was over, I handed him the book. He read it and told me: 'I think it's great, and I hope you get it. But no matter who gets it, I'm gonna play that part.'"

—Michael Wayne

John Wayne's Rooster Cogburn eye patch and personal copy of Charles Portis's novel *True Grit*.

John Wayne as
Robert Hightower in
3 Godfathers (1948).

NEVER GIVE UP

In *3 Godfathers* (1948), John Wayne plays Robert Hightower, a bank robber on the run with his two partners. In the desert, the three men encounter a woman who is dying after giving birth. The men vow to get the newborn to safety, but Hightower's partners soon fall to the hardships of the desert. Undeterred, Hightower continues on and finally, thanks to his unyielding determination, he makes it to town, where the baby is taken in by a family. The film is a reminder that quitting is simply not an option when others are counting on you.

"My feeling about life is that you're put here and you have to make your own way."

—John Wayne

John Wayne as the Ringo Kid in *Stagecoach* (1939).

John Wayne, Ken Curtis, Dan Dailey and Tige Andrews in *The Wings of Eagles* (1957).

WORK WITH WHAT YOU HAVE

The Wings of Eagles was only allotted 47 days for shooting, but Duke made the most of his time by turning in a classic performance.

WHERE THERE'S A WILL, THERE'S A WAY

In 1957, John Wayne starred in *The Wings of Eagles*, a film based on the life of director John Ford's friend Frank "Spig" Wead. Following an accident that leaves him partially paralyzed, Wead is forced to leave his career as a Navy pilot and venture into a new career as a screenwriter. His passion for flying never fades, though, and he remains determined to find his way back into a cockpit. In one of the film's most inspiring scenes, Wead's trainer "Jughead" Carson (Dan Dailey) rallies the paralyzed pilot by having him chant, "I'm gonna move that toe!" The scene is a reminder that sometimes, the most impossible dreams can begin to take flight with a simple statement.

"When he was dying of cancer in the hospital, he was in an extreme amount of pain. But he never ever complained about the suffering he was going through—so much so, my brothers and sisters and I at times thought, 'He's gonna beat this despite what the doctors say.' We kept up hope. He was more focused on helping those in the hospital around him who were suffering, trying to give them hope and encouragement. He demonstrated so much courage, which was always something that marked him, but this was the greatest demonstration of it for me."

—Patrick Wayne

Duke and Patrick Wayne in Hollywood, California.

John Wayne and
Ethan on the set of
*The Sons of Katie
Elder* (1965).

AGE IS JUST A NUMBER

"I was 10 when he was 66 years old. [And] he's on a horse, he's running at full speed across open country with a herd of horses running with him.... He was a bold, outgoing individual who was full of life, constantly moving forward.... And nobody sits on a horse like John Wayne does."

—Ethan Wayne

John Wayne accepts his first and only Academy Award for Best Actor on April 7, 1970.

GRATITUDE

Duke made sure to constantly convey just how thankful he was for the life that he lived.

"We lived a very nice, comfortable life. But I remember wanting a Ringo Starr record, it was like $5.99, and he said, 'No, we just spent some money, I think that's a little too much for today.' And then after I did some chores, he ended up going and getting it for me and surprising me with it. He was very generous, but he also wanted us to be aware that stuff doesn't just appear out of thin air—you have to work for it. And when you do work for it, you end up appreciating it even more."

—Marisa Wayne

John Wayne holds his daughter Marisa.

REWARD A DAY'S WORK

Marisa Wayne recalls that when her father picked her up from school, he would often treat her to popcorn or ice cream.

Duke and Ethan
Wayne on the set
of the 1967 film
The War Wagon.

"By the time I came along, he was aging. But because his fan base was so strong, he was still able to play parts as a leading man. And he was constantly grateful that he could still make movies. I can't remember a meal where he wasn't interrupted, but he would always be gracious and take time to speak to the people. He was familiar to them, even though they weren't familiar to him. He had a lot of gratitude for the people who allowed him to continue to make films."

—Ethan Wayne

A GIFT SHOWS YOUR GRATITUDE

Each time John Wayne finished shooting a film, he would give his coworkers a special memento before parting ways. Each and every member of the cast and the crew received a custom coffee mug featuring the film's title and a beautiful illustration, which Duke paid for out of pocket. More than a fun vessel from which to sip a cup of joe, the mugs were John Wayne's way of letting his coworkers know they were just as integral to the project as he was. He knew no matter how big or small the gesture, the sentiment of gratitude was what mattered.

Walter Brennan, Patrick
Wayne and John Wayne
on the set of *Rio Bravo*
(1959). Inset: The film's
commemorative mug.

John Wayne with his wife Pilar and son Ethan on the set of *The Sons of Katie Elder* (1965).

BE SELFLESS

"You'd never know he had only one lung and a bad knee and had been falling off horses for six decades. He never stopped being John Wayne, even when he was sick—and the work wasn't easy for him.

He did what he was expected to do because he had kids who were depending on him to keep a roof over their heads and film crews who needed him to stay employed. He worried more about others than himself."

—Ethan Wayne

TAKE TIME
TO BE KIND

For as unfathomably busy as he always
was, John Wayne still managed to
make time for the people responsible
for the ongoing success of his career.
The star would receive endless
amounts of fan mail, and he made
the effort to personally reply to the
adoring public as much as possible.
Duke also realized stepping out into
public meant being swarmed by
people hoping to get an autograph,
which is why he carried cards bearing
his signature to easily hand out to
everyone who came up to him.
When it comes to expressing your
gratitude, no gesture is ever too small.

John Wayne signs autographs for a group of fans.

ALWAYS BE PREPARED

According to Duke's youngest son Ethan, the legend often carried pre-autographed cards with him to hand out to fans when he went in public.

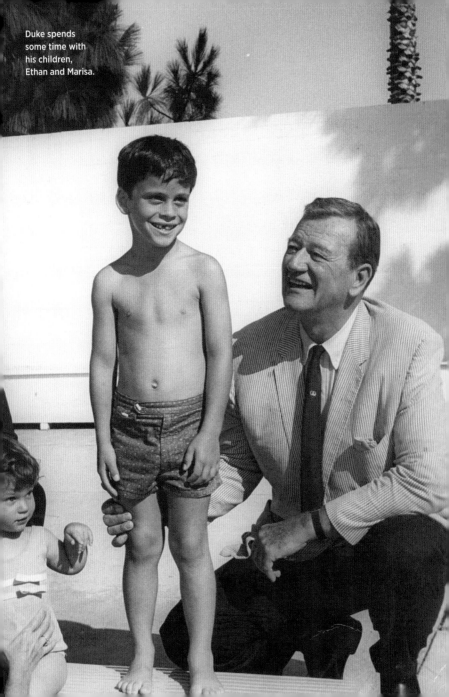

Duke spends some time with his children, Ethan and Marisa.

"Unfortunately, financially he wasn't always well taken care of. Maybe people treated him poorly in certain business decisions or whatever it may be, but he wasn't small or petty.
He wouldn't take the time to go back and try and deal with things in a legal sense.
He preferred to just leave it behind and move forward.
His idea was 'OK, that happened, but do I want to spend six or seven months dealing with it, or do I want to just move on and enjoy my life going forward?'
I think there's grace in that."

—Ethan Wayne

"When he was at home, there was always fan mail. And he liked to correspond; he was always signing photographs and sending them. He tried to answer every piece of fan mail—and he got a lot of it—because he had a ton of respect for the people who took the time to write. There were a couple occasions when we'd be out surrounded by fans and I'd say, 'Dad, doesn't this bother you?' and he'd say, 'No honey, without these people I wouldn't have a job.'"

—Marisa Wayne

Marisa, Patrick and other Wayne family members at the opening of the John Wayne Cancer Institute in Los Angeles, c. 1981.

AYNE CANCER CLINIC

DUKE'S LEGACY LIVES ON

The John Wayne Cancer Foundation continues to make strides in research and awareness today through various campaigns.

GIVE BACK
WHENEVER POSSIBLE

"He didn't want to be president or have things named after him. He knew he had to be famous because that's how you got your movies made. But he was actually very humble. When he was dying, he turned to my late brother Michael and said: 'Whatever you do, use my name for the benefit of the public. If it weren't for the public, I wouldn't be here; you wouldn't be here. We wouldn't have had the life we had.' And that was the beginning of the John Wayne Cancer Foundation."

—Melinda Wayne

LET 'EM LEARN BY YOUR SIDE

Patrick Wayne co-starred with his father in several classics including *The Searchers* (1956), *McLintock!* (1963) and *Big Jake* (1971).

AFTERWORD

By Patrick Wayne

When my siblings and I got to spend quality time with our father, whether it was on Catalina Island, at home or on the boat, it always ended up being a big competition for his attention because there were so many of us. But I ended up getting a little bit of a break because as we were growing up, I was the only one who expressed any interest in working in film. So, I got to have a lot of additional special time with him. I hadn't decided at the age of nine that I was going to work in acting—I did it because it was a chance to spend time with my dad without having to compete with my brothers and sisters.

As far as acting, he never really gave me advice or lessons. He wasn't an advice-offering type of person in general. Instead, he operated by example. Everything I learned from him was by example.

I have four grown children of my own now, and just as my dad did, I knew I had to lead by example as I raised them. You can try to tell kids so many important things but if you don't live according to those lessons yourself, there's no point because they're not going to follow anything you say. Which is why I've tried to be a beacon for whatever I express. And

I've lucked out with my kids—I have two attorneys, an investment banker and my youngest son is working on his masters in biochemistry—so they all turned out great. And I'm taking full credit for that because you always get blamed if they turn out poorly!

I'm proud of them. I know dad would be too. And I also know he'd take pride in knowing that the ideals he championed will be passed on to you and your kids.

And who wouldn't want to make John Wayne proud?

—PATRICK WAYNE

Media Lab Books
For inquiries, call 646-838-6637

Copyright 2020 Topix Media Lab

Published by Topix Media Lab
14 Wall Street, Suite 4B
New York, NY 10005

Manufactured in Singapore

ISBN-13: 978-1-948174-43-5
ISBN-10: 1-948174-43-X

CEO Tony Romando

Vice President & Publisher Phil Sexton
Senior Vice President of Sales & New Markets Tom Mifsud
Vice President of Retail Sales & Logistics Linda Greenblatt
Director of Finance Vandana Patel
Manufacturing Director Nancy Puskuldjian
Financial Analyst Matthew Quinn
Brand Marketing & Promotions Assistant Emily McBride

Editor-in-Chief Jeff Ashworth
Creative Director Steven Charny
Photo Director Dave Weiss
Managing Editor Courtney Kerrigan
Senior Editor Tim Baker

Content Editor Trevor Courneen
Content Designer Kelsey Payne
Art Director Susan Dazzo
Associate Photo Editor Catherine Armanasco
Associate Editor Juliana Sharaf
Copy Editors & Fact Checkers Benjamin VanHoose, Tara Sherman

Co-Founders Bob Lee, Tony Romando

JOHN WAYNE
ENTERPRISES